19 ways to make money on

INSTAGRAM

ROXANNE MARTIN

ROXANNE MARTIN

ISBN: 978-1717180216

Table of Contents

Introduction

Instagram is a mobile, desktop, and Internet-based photo-sharing application and service that allows users to share pictures and videos either publicly, or privately to pre-approved followers. Instagram is a simple way to capture and share the world's moments. Follow your friends and family to see what they're up to, and discover accounts from all over the world that are sharing things you love.

This is the kind of book that is a must read for you if you want to work and make money with your Instagram account as it enlightens you on how to use your account beyond just posting pictures for likes and comments. With this book you will learn how to start keeping a great Instagram profile and how to monetize it.

With over 2.8 billion active users in 2017 worldwide, social media has become a terrific channel for businesses to connect with their customers, build brand awareness, and improve their marketing strategy.

And, if your target audience loves visuals, then you cannot afford to ignore the platform that sees 80 million photo updates every day...

Instagram is a force of nature and Pretty impressive. What was merely a photo-sharing app initially has become one of the top social media platforms in less than seven years.

It has quickly doubled its user base in the last two years to 700 million users. Its growth has exploded since it launched Instagram Stories in August 2016

In particular, businesses belonging to the fashion, travel, or food industry have a terrific opportunity to engage with their audience on the app you can download for free -Instagram.

Yet, only 30% of businesses are active on social media have an Instagram account. You might think that low business adoption rate will mean that you'll face lower competition and see higher social engagement and more free Instagram followers.

Chapter 1: Where to start

Building a great profile

Instagram is deceptive. There appears to be nothing to it: take a picture, upload it, and throw on a hashtag or two.

However, as anyone who has tried the above approach knows, simply using Instagram's basic features doesn't lend itself to tons of followers or hundreds of likes.

The perfect Instagram profile will look different for each person. But whether you're looking to become Insta-famous, want to cultivate a specialized following, or just want to get a few more likes on your selfie, there are a few strategies that apply no matter what.

With just a few tweaks to your profile, you can greatly increase your number of followers and likes. Once you get the hang of them, the extra steps are second nature. Take a few moments now to double-check your Instagram profile to ensure you're on the path to popularity.

Getting the Basics Down

The minute you start setting up your account, you have to start making smart decisions about the foundational pieces of any strong Instagram profile.

1. Choose a user name: You have two names on Instagram: your username (@YourUsername) and a changeable name that displays alongside your handle in searches. Given the millions of users on Instagram, it's hard to find a unique username, but try as hard as possible to use one without strange characters or spellings. This helps other users remember it and tag you more

easily. It's best if you directly associate your changeable name with either your name or brand so that people can find you through search.

2. Set your visibility: If you want to gain popularity on Instagram, you must set your profile to public. Otherwise, no one will see anything that you post except for friends from other social networks. That said, some users choose to change their profile back to private after they gain a certain number of followers.

3. Select your profile photo: For a personal account, a clear headshot of your face is generally best. For brands or companies, try a recognizable product or logo so followers know who you are. If people can't recognize you or your company from your profile photo, it's unlikely they will follow you.

Crafting a Perfect Bio

Your bio is only 150 characters, but it sets the tone for your entire profile. If you want people to notice you, it's important to get it right!

Most importantly, your bio should give a brief overview of who you are and what your profile is about. Using single words to describe yourself (e.g., "Author," "Photographer," "Runner") and your location is always a great place to start. You can also add a hashtag or two so your profile will show up in searches, or ask your followers to use a specific hashtag so that you can see their posts.

Depending on what your profile is all about, you may want to add a short sentence explaining its purpose. Are you collecting pictures of pugs? Photographing every tree on your route to school? Trying to sell shoes? Let your potential followers know what they're getting into by following you.

One trend to be careful of: emojis.

A picture is worth a thousand words, but depending on the type of profile you want, emojis may not be the best choice. If your Instagram is focused on a serious art project or brand, avoid emojis. If, on the other hand, your Instagram is lighthearted and trendy, a few carefully chosen emojis might go over well with your audience.

Lastly, your bio is the only place on Instagram where you can add a hyperlink to another website. If you want to direct traffic elsewhere from your profile, this is the place to do it. You can add additional website addresses directly in your bio. But only the one you set as your official website will appear as an actual hyperlink.

Choosing a niche

Before you can even start building your Internet business, you will need to choose a niche to build your business around. After all, you cannot build any kind of business if you do not know what that business will be about.

Many marketers say that you should choose a niche that you are passionate about. However, I don't think that is necessarily true. Just think about it for a few minutes.

What are you passionate about? How many other people are passionate about the same thing? Maybe you are passionate about gardening. Great! That would be a good niche to build your business around as there are hundreds of thousands, more likely millions of people interested in gardening. But if you are passionate about some obscure subject, how many people do you think have a passion for the same thing? Probably very few so how can you expect to make any money in that particular niche?

Think about it logically. Just being passionate about something may not be enough to build a profitable business around. In order to be successful, your chosen niche must have enough profit potential that you can actually make money in it. Otherwise, it will be just a hobby, not an actual business.

PLEASE NOTE: According to the IRS, if your business does not become profitable within a couple of years, then it is a hobby, not a business. And, the IRS does not allow tax deductions for hobbies. Choosing a profitable niche is the first step to building a profitable business instead of a hobby.

On the other hand, if you have absolutely no interest or very little interest in a niche, it will be very hard for you to work in that niche. Never choose a niche just because you think you can make a lot of money in it, especially if you do not have much interest in it.

If you choose a niche you have no interest in, you will end up making excuses for why you cannot work that day. You won't want to spend time creating products to promote to your subscribers. Without any products, you will not make any money in that niche. Plus, you'll have a hard time coming up with ideas to write articles about. Without articles, you have no content to send to your subscribers.

Since your subscribers joined your list because they thought you would help them solve their problems, you'll never be able to maintain your list of subscribers if you never send them the information they want.

So you will end up starting all over again in a different niche, wasting all of the time, effort and money you spent in a niche you end up abandoning. If you have some interest in a niche, it will be much easier for you to do the many tasks associated with building a profitable online business around that niche. So, whatever niche you chose should be something you are at least interested in or something you want to learn more about.

So, you really don't need to be passionate about the niche you choose but you do need to have some interest in it. While your ultimate goal is to make money, you will still need to choose a niche that you will enjoy working in.

In order to be successful, you can't be a small fish in a big ocean. All small fish either get eaten or they become lost in the vast numbers of larger fish.

You will need to do some research to find a niche which you can narrow down into one or more profitable sub-niches. You need to choose a sub-niche with a high demand for the products you will be creating and which also offers a large number of products you can promote

Getting more followers

You can't ignore the power of Instagram. It's a social media giant and a fantastic place for businesses and brands to connect with their followers and maximize sales.

But for every person or business that has a big, receptive following, there are thousands more that don't. Instagram can be powerful, but you have to be smart about how you use it.

Share Eye-Catching Images:

Instagram is a photo sharing site. So, above all else, you want more followers on Instagram invest some time ensuring that your pictures are really good. Also post content that is interesting, as well as photos that are well-composed and eye-catching.

Like Photos:

Don't forget, Instagram is a social network so it's important to interact with others. To get more Instagram followers start by liking plenty of pictures in your market to get people interested in following you. Leaving comments also helps. But ensure that they're genuine and not spammy! And don't forget to follow accounts you like, too!

Time Your Pictures Right:

Research shows that the best time to post on Instagram is at 5pm on Wednesdays. This may or may not be correct for your page. Based upon on your niche, the demographics of your followers and other things specific to your niche and content, Wednesday might or might not be a good day for you.Finding the best time to post for your audience takes time to learn so track the likes and comments on each photo, and start looking for any trends occurring different times of the day.

Use Hashtags:

Using the right hashtags can really help you to gain followers on Instagram. Many people search out certain hashtags, and your images have that hashtag, it will be there waiting for them. Hashtags can help your content reach a broad range of people that may have nothing to do with your account, in other words they don't follow you specifically. By simply using some hashtags, you can increase your content's reach significantly.

Host A Contest:

 Post an amusing or fascinating photo to your account and offer a prize to a follower who comes up with the best caption. Use apps like Heyo, WishPond and AgoraPulse to run your contest.

Link To Other Social Networks:

If you have followers on other social media channels like Facebook, Twitter or Pinterest, invite those people to follow you on Instagram. Make it be easy for people to connect with you in multiple places.

 Instagram has over 700 million active monthly users and its popularity continues to rocket, as the cameras in smart phones become better at taking high-quality pics and videos.

Engaging with the audience

It's probably one of the most frustrating parts of social media marketing — no engagement.

You post day in and day out hoping to see the social side of social media start to happen. Sometimes, a like or two will pop up, but most of the time, you hear crickets. It's disheartening. It's also costly. Your social media marketing can't pay off if your audience isn't getting excited about what you have to say.

Social media is a popular way to use direct marketing. This type of marketing allows you to connect one-on-one with your customer, speaking directly to the person who will eventually open his wallet and buy from you.

No doubt, the most effective way of gaining tremendous and quick social recognition on Instagram is to appear in the "Most Popular" list.

Imagine the Instagram team sends you a congratulation message and soon after that your number of followers rapidly increases. The feeling of making it to the "Most Popular" list in Instagram will be quite exciting.

You might be wondering how to make it to Instagram's "most popular" list. If you want to become a "most popular" in Instagram, then you should consider the following strategies. What is the Secret Formula to Become an Instagram "Most Popular" Member?

Instagram's "Most Populars" algorithm is not really known although the amount of "likes" seems to be an important factor. Your chances of appearing in the "Most Popular" will increase the more likes you get as quickly as possible.

You will most likely become a part of this valued chart once you receive lots of "Likes".

This means that the most fundamental and important criterion is the number of followers. Nonetheless, it is also equally important that you work on your profile with genuine interest.

Just like Twitter, following a lot of people on Instagram is the easiest way of having "followers" and in return, a certain number of them will add to you too. Nonetheless, keep in mind that doing good work, being constant and patient is the most natural way of getting new followers.

How to promote your Instagram profile

1. Who you are: Use your original name and nickname, which are easy to mention and remember.

2. Your profile picture: If you are not an extremely handsome guy or a good-looking girl, there are still a few tricks you can use to make your profile picture stand out.

3. Some other elements that you promote your profile include humanity, humility and humor.

Boost yourself to the "Most Populars"

1. Picture quality: Be creative, original and spend time editing.

2. Picture information: Give your pictures a human touch, titles and use effects.

3. Where is it? : Link Instagram account to Foursquare and Geo-Tag your pictures.

4. Transmit knowledge to your users: Add value to the lives of your users and they will follow you with more interest.

5. Put interest in your users: If you want a bigger group of friends, be ready to spend more time communicating with your community.

6. Be original by using emoticons in your comments and nicks.

7. Organize original contests: It's good but can take lots of time.

8. "Hits" are worth celebrating! Never forget to thank and congratulate your followers.

Remember there are over one million Instagramers in the world. Do not forget, Instagram is a global app and your location is very important in your attempt to become the most popular on Instagram.

If you are from a country like Japan or USA, where Instagram is massively used, you will have higher chances of entering the "Most Populars" ranking. Along with location, the time you post is equally important to get followers. Soon enough, Instagram might also start taking different countries, different thematics, and more local factors into consideration when creating a "Most Popular" ranking. This might not have happened yet, but can be expected in the near future.

If you want local followers from your time zone, then you should post in the morning while they are awake but still in bed, and/or at night when they are headed to bed. Users tend to check their Instagram account and other social network profiles at these times. Then again, if you want to make it to the "Most Populars" list, you will also have to focus on followers from all around the world.

Good photos and patience!

If you want one of your photos to appear in the Instagram "most popular" list, then you will have to work hard and be patient. Patience is not just a virtue but will turn out to become the key to being rated "Most Popular".

To be patient you will also have to learn to be dedicated as well. To become "most popular" on Instagram, you will also have to start thinking and helping others as well. You cannot create a network in just a single shot!

Being ranked into the "Most Popular" list on Instagram is certainly an accomplishment worth bragging, but to get there you will have to make an effort, and it will take time.

Chapter 2 - How to monetize your Instagram account

1.Open a Shopify account.

Shopify is an online store builder that provides you with anything from hosting, domain, so that anyone can sell online. With Shopify, you won't have to worry about server, security or any other technical issues. You just need to sign up an account to open a store, then take care of the content of your store. Currently there are over 250,000 stores using Shopify to sell online.

With that being said, Shopify is great for, but not limited to, small and medium business owners, especially who have little to no coding skills. Though, many coders/developers still come to Shopify as the best choice because they are free from technical issues and can invest all resources into products, marketing and selling.

What may bother you is Shopify pricing. Shopify is a premium service, which means there is no free plan, only a free trial for 14 days, and then you are bound to buy one of the packages. Also, for Basic Shopify stores, you are charged 2% for each transaction.

A shopify store is one of the most common ways of making money on Instagram, by placing the link to your website in the Instagram profile. As long as your audience is bult on the same niche as your Shopify store, you can start making money right away.

2.Sell an intellectual product.

After properly setting your account and get some followers, you should consider promoting intellectual products to your audience. This is a great idea because you can make money right away as an influencer and you can also see how your audience reacts to different products. This experience will help you understand the audience, what they like, what they are willing to pay for and what they are not willing to pay for. When you are confident enough that you know what your audience responds to, you can start developing your own products to promote. This will bring you more money then other people's products and from there you can start expanding your brand by creating other products. Intellectual products are a great idea because they are easy to update and you don't have to worry about shipping costs.

3.Write a book and promote it.

As mentioned in the previous step, after promoting other people's books and products, you now can write your own book on the topic. This will not be very hard since you must already have some quality photos for your niche and some content, which you used when building your audience. You just new to come op with a few fresh articles and pack all of it in one book or even a series of books.

4.Write an app and promote it.

An app is always build to solve a problem. You must have some ideas of problems that need to be resolved in your niche. In case you don't have a great idea of an app for your niche, you can always ask your audience about the challenges they face when working in that field or doing that passion related to your niche.

Building an app sounds scary but is not. The hardest thing about building an app is coming up with a specific concept. There are many developers online who would be willing to build your app for anything from $100/£100. The only reason why they don't have an app business is because they don't have any ideas about what type of app to build. They have probably tried once of twice and have been unsuccessful so they decided to build apps for someone else. This happened because you need to be an expert in your field or to do proper research before deciding if the app could become successful. So you need to have a very specific idea in mind when going to a developer. A sketch of what the app should look like and how it would work.

5.Test product ideas on them.

Testing a product is vital part of the research for any successful business. This step might be hard to do when the business is a startup or in the process of opening and has no audience. This is where you come in place. If the business is targeting people like the ones forming your audience, your Instagram account can be used to tell if the product they have in mind is a go or no go. Of course you could also test your own products, but testing other people's products can make you money instantly. Keep in mind that you need to negotiate before agreeing to use your hard earned followers for other businesses. Make sure you do your homework about how much other influencers are charging and how many followers they have. There are different ways to test products. You can ask them to fill a quick survey or just to make a list of top 3 things they would change in a product similar to the one your business is thinking of. Sometimes the business have too may options and needs your audience to tell them what would sell more. For example the business has three different models of tent and doesn't know which one to choose.

6. Send your audience to affiliate products.

There are may products that you can promote within a niche, but the most important part is to keep your audience's trust, by promoting things that you have tested and used and you actually believe that are very good. If you have an account that is focusing on traveling, you can find products related to traveling, like smaller versions of items (small scissors, shampoo bottles), or maybe you find some really good traveling kits that have many items inside that people need while traveling. Good paces to find affiliate products are affiliate program websites. For each niche there are some specific websites to get affiliate products. If you want to promote a specific product, you can contact the company and express your interest. Don't forget to negotiate your rates.

7. Use your account to promote an event

A great way to get new customers for a business is by organizing an event, free (meet up or webinar) or paid (workshop or mini course).

People love an event, that's where they can make new connections, enjoy an experience and get to communicate, have their questions answered and even learn new skills. When you make an impact on people's lives and give them a good experience they go and tell their friends about it and that's how you can expand you audience too.

8. Use your audience to send followers to other social media platforms.

If having thousands of followers on Instagram makes you money, you can send them to your Youtube Channel or your Facebook account. Now you have two accounts that you can monetize in different ways, so you can charge people more to promote their products on different platforms and you can test and sell your products on your other platforms too.

9. Use the audience to find a better-paid job

Having an impressive Instagram account will look good in your resume and would make a difference between a yes and a no in a job interview process. Once you Instagarm account has thousands of followers, people are going to start notice you.
You will start getting email about affiliates, business proposals and even job offers. Once you prove that you can manage your account and monetize it well, you could apply and get a job as a Social Media Manager, or anything that you are passionate about.

10. Sell your Instagram photos

There are many ways to sell photos. You can make a photography book and publish it, or maybe a coloring book out of them by hiring to turn them into cartoons. You can sell your books in kindle or CreateSpace.

Upload your Instagram photos on photography websites.
You can also upload them in stock photography websites like
iStockPhoto, ShutterStock, Adobe Stock, Big Stock Photo. You
will need a high number of quality photos in your account.

11. Organize a competition to promote products.

People love a good competition. You can organize this to
promote, sell your products or to get reviews. Another way you
can use a good competition is by promoting an affiliate product
and ask the business to provide the price, so you are only
acting as a middle man. See what item is in high demand ex:
Kindle fire and offer it as a prize. You can make everything
transparent, like choosing the winner and film the event, so
the users get more engaged and confident about future
competitions.

12. Get reviews

You cando this for yourself of ask your audience to rate other
products. Use freelance websites like Fiverr to find people who
need reviews. Reviews are essential to any product, they can
be use to increase the value of the product or to find out how
the product can be improved. Thinking of a good way to
monetize this aspect of a business, you can contact people from
E-bay and Amazon who are selling products with few reviews
in your niche and make them an offer. This would only work
out for them if they have a quality product.

13. Get paid per share

The freelance websites and influencer ones have offers where you can charge per share, regardless of the platform. If you have expanded your audience to Facebook or Youtube, as mentioned in the previous step, you can now charge for both platforms. My advice is to focus on Instagram at first. Once you reach 100K followers, you can charge between $5-$100 depending on the niche and the gain brought to the client.

14. Post adds and get paid

The adds you can charge for can be about letting you audience know about a new business, a great TED talk or Youtube video. It can also be about a hot new invention in your niche or a cool app that has just been launched, anything goes al song as you can charge for it and it's good quality.

15. Charge for surveys

Surveys can be use for anything. You can help a sociology student to a research study (for a small fee). You can do that for a business or even for yourself. Make sure that you do your market research about what other influencers with a similar number of followers charge.

16. Help a business find an employee

Think about acting like an employment agency. A business needs an employee in the field that your audience is built in and. You can find these businesses advertising their job in the local newspaper or job websites. Get in touch with them and offer to promote their add and maybe charge a fee for the add or if they find the right person through your services, you can charge them as much as an employment agency. Your audience is not just in one city so you can check where most of your audience is from and focus on those specific cities when looking for companies that need employees.

17. Help an aspiring influencer

An influencer might contact you with fewer followers than you have and you can charge them for sending followers their way. Make sure that the people what you work with have accounts in similar niches, but not the same. You don't want them as competitors. This is also a great way of getting new followers. You might not want to charge them a fee, if they have a high number of followers in a similar niche, you might want to exchange services, they promote something about your Instagram account and you do the same for them. This still rings you money but indirectly, because once your account is bigger, you can charge more for all the services mentioned so far.

18. Open a consultancy business

You can make a massive change for a business if you give them the right answers to questions related to their audience. You can easily get in touch with them and offer your consultancy services to help with:

-To research if a business ideas in good and if people are willing to pay for it.

-To improve a product that is already on the market.

-To find the right price range for a product.

If you know how to build a website, that would be even better. You can write about all the way you can improve their business and all the services you offer through your Instagram account. They can go on your website and send enquiries and you can get back to them with an offer.

19. Charity fundraising

This is a great way to make money but maybe not for

yourself, but for others. You can recommend a charity to your audience and encourage them to donate to it for a cause that you believe in. Giving is as important as receiving and if you use your Instagram account for this, I am a firm believer that is going to come back to you.

Chapter 3 - How to keep your Instagram account

Since I run Instagram account, I'm active everyday checking out the feeds of small businesses, handmade brands, and indie-preneur's trying to grow their businesses. Every day I cringe at the simple tweaks they could be making to their Instagram accounts that would just open the floodgates for growth and engagement.

Being a fairly new platform on the marketing scene, there are a lot of businesses not sure why their posts aren't getting them more followers and engagement that translates into sales. So how can you make sure you're using this viral social media platform to it's fullest marketing potential?

Well, we've managed to grow our Instagram account followers, in just few months. You can have that same kind of serious growth too. Not tooting our own horn here, but since we've mastered it, I wanted to share my best tips with you to grow your audience.

Mistakes to avoid

1. There's No Link in Bio to Drive Traffic

Of all the mistakes you can make as a brand on IG, not including a link in your bio is one of, if not THE HUGEST. Instagram gives you a whole space dedicated for a hyperlink (that means people can click it) so USE IT! Link to your store or a particular product page if you're running a sale for example.

The easier you make it for followers to find your store, the more traffic you will get.

2. There's No Description in Your Bio – Or It Just Sucks

What defines a sucky bio description? Boring , all about you, only about your products.

What's even worse? NOT HAVING ONE AT ALL. It makes you look unprofessional.

What defines an epic bio description? Describes the "why" or mission/philosophy behind your products. Concisely describes what you do/sell. Here are some steps to learn how to craft the perfect social media bio.

3. Crappy Resolution Photos Are Scaring Away Potential Customers

Think of it this way… the higher the resolution, the higher your level of professionality. Or at least that's how it looks on IG. So take advantage of that. No matter how big your brand is, you should look totes professional if you want sales.

Here's a lil trick. Make the resolution of your photo 2x the recommended size so when it gets compressed it still looks fab. So for IG, your images should be 1280px by 1280 px.

4. Your Photos Aren't Sized Right

If your images aren't the right size (or shape – they should be square!) then your awesome products get cropped funny and important stuff gets cut out.

So make sure:

1. Your images are 1280px by 1280px and

2. Keep the square orientation in mind when taking your photos.

If you have non-square images that you don't want to crop, you can use an app like Instasize (for iPhone) (for Android) to properly size them for Instagram.

5. Terrible Lighting is Downgrading Your Image

And when I say 'image" here, I mean literally your photo, and also the look of your brand. Good lighting is the difference between looking like a tween taking crappy cell-phone pics and a pro shooting for Anthropologie catalogs. Let's make sure you're the second

6. Where the Ever-Important Lifestyle Photos At?

Like mentioned before, it's not enough to just have product photos. Those are good for focusing on product details, but you ALSO need lifestyle photos showing your products in use. Why? Because they give context and your customers will be able to imagine themselves using your products! If they can't imagine themselves using them, there's no way they will spend their moolah on them.

7. All Your Posts Look Exactly the Same

I see a lot of newbie feeds that are just photo after photo of basically the same thing. You have to think about how your feed looks as a whole, not just as individual pictures showing up in your followers' feeds. You have to keep things interesting or your followers will have no reason to keep following you. It's okay if your products all look similar, or if you only offer one kind of product. Your job is to make things more visually interesting by mixing up your posts.

Photograph your products with different backgrounds.

Add lifestyle photos.

Incorporate other content that's relevant to your audience (not necessarily product photos).

8. You're Posting Inconsistently

I see a lot of people who are too sporadic with their posting habits. The most common thing I see is that someone will be super active and post 3x per day for a week, and then drop off the face of the Earth for a month. You can't do this! Your followers need to know what to expect from you!

So being consistent it key. 1-2 posts per day is solid... as long as you do it every day!

9. You're Posting At All the Wrong Times

It's super simple.Don't post when your people aren't on Instagram! Post when they ARE. (PST, there is no one BEST time to post. It varies from business to business, from audience to audience).

If you aren't sure when your audience is most active, test out some different times of day. Then use Iconosquare to view your statistics. It will show you which posts did the best, and when your optimal times are for posting.

10. Less-than Engaging Copy Isn't Strengthening Your Images

The copy you write in your descriptions is the 2nd most important thing to your post behind your images. Your copy should supplement your image and back it up with any relevant and important info you can't include in your images.

If more engagement is what you're looking for, then try asking a question. But make sure you ask a DIRECT question, not an open-ended question. If the answer is in the question, you'll get way more answers from your peeps.

Direct Question = Would you buy blue or black?

Open-ended Question = What do you think?

11. Your Copy is Way Too Long & Distracting

I was checking out someone's feed one time and clicked on a super cute photo ('cause I mean, it was super cute) but the second I had to scroll to read the novel-length description I immediately clicked away. I can't even tell you what the image was for... I was too turned off by the hella-long "omg this project was so special to me" speech written under it.

Your post descriptions are not meant to be long! Keep them as short as you can while still offering the essential information and a little bit of pizazz... or you'll lose people just like that.

Rule of Thumb: Don't make your peeps have to scroll to read!

12. There Ain't No Call-to-Action in Your Copy

IF you want your followers to do something, you're gonna have to flat out tell them. Even if it seems overly-obvious to you... it may not be to everyone. So don't let potential customers fall through the cracks by not directing them.

If you want them to visit your store, say "Click the link in bio to shop this look!".

13. Being Too Salesy & Killing the Fun, Social (and Beneficial) Part of Instagram Marketing

The number one turn off for potential followers is directly asking them to follow you or buy when you're personally engaging. Whatever you do, DO NOT EVER respond to comments with:

"Follow me, I'll follow back!" , "Buy it in my Etsy store here…"

"It'd be great if you could shout me out!"

Car salesmen have the rep of being obnoxious for a reason. People love to buy, but they hate being sold. It's okay to use a Call-to-Action as mentioned in Tip 12 if your post is promoting a product (you need to give them enough info so they CAN buy if they choose to) but when you're engaging in comments, you should keep things lighter and more personable.

14. Not Using Hashtags for Exposure

Instagram posts with 11+ hashtags get the most interaction. That's because they don't just get buried under your more recent posts, but are archived in the hashtag group they are tagged in where people can find them forever.

Let's say you tag your photo with #inspiration. If anyone clicks on any #inspiration hashtag or searches #inspiration, your photo will show up with any others that also use the hashtag. Like this:

Do some hashtag research on Iconosquare to find the relevant ones to your audience and post 4-5 as a comment on your posts. After 30 minutes, delete that comment and write a new one with 4-5 new relevant hashtags. This way you get the exposure of lots of hashtags without looking spammy.

15. Irrelevant Content Turns Away the Right Audience

Always, ALWAYS post content for your audience and no one else. No matter how much you love that hilarious llama picture, if it has nothing to do with your audience then JUST SAY NO.

If you post the content your target audience wants to see, those are the kinds of people that will follow you – not just llama lovers. And when you build a strong, relevant audience, that's when you can convert them to CU$TOMER$.

16. You're Running Contests When You Don't Have an Audience Yet

Instagram contests are a great way to boost engagement and excitement about your products but, I'm just gonna be honest with you... if you only have 80 followers, a contest isn't going to do you any good right now.

The last thing you want is to run a contest and get more cricket chirps than entries... it will make your feed look kinda sad. So right now, focus on growing your Instagram audience before you try running a contest, and then hit it hard when you have the right audience!

17. Expecting Followers to Just Come to You

Unless you already have a well-known, highly searched brand, then chances are your Instagram account won't just be found by potential followers. It's up to you to bring them to you. How do you do that? You find them first!

Use the hashtags your followers use because then your

images will be categorized with the photos they are already posting and looking at... TA DA they can find you there.

   Search those hashtags and comment on the people that use them (theoretically these should be your target audience). Write nice comments, "Diggin' this photo!", etc. They will appreciate the fact that you found them and took the time to engage with them... and that appreciation often translates to followers.

18. Your Incohesive Look Makes Your Brand Unrecognizable

When you think about bigger brands like Nike, Anthropologie, Urban Outfitters, you imagine a certain look and vibe, and that's a huge part of how you recognize them. The reason they are recognizable is because they have a cohesive look. You need your brand to be recognizable, and be considered as professional as the bigger brands – so you need a cohesive look for your Instagram.

19. Why Are There Selfies? It's NOT About You

No joke, I've seen way too many brand feeds with selfies. If that's you... please stop! It's one thing if you're Marie Forleo and have built a brand around your persona (because then your face on your Instagram makes sense) but if you are a product based business, selfies really have no place here. Remember, ALL your content is about your AUDIENCE, not you.

20. Following Way More People Than Follow You

Some people think that if you follow someone, they'll follow you back. That'd be great, but it's really not the case. So if you are following 5,000 people and only have 500 followers, that makes you look bad. You want to look credible, and your followers let others know that they go to YOU for your content... not the other way around.

21. You're Not Using Geo-tags for an Engagement Boost!

A cool option each of your posts has is to include a geo-location tag, basically to tell your followers where you are posting from. Posts using a geo-tag get 79% more engagement. This is PERFECT ammo for anyone that goes to events.

Say you're at Renegade in Los Angeles... geo-tag that shizz! Let everyone know exactly where you are. Or if you're at a networking event, geo-tag your post and other cool people you'd like to meet will see where you'll be.

Whatever you do, don't post blindly.

If you keep these mistakes in mind and avoid them at all costs, your posts will be primed for growing exposure, more followers, and increased sales!

Things That Could Make Instagram Shot Down your Account

This happens more often than you'd think, and you don't have to be famous, or even Internet famous, to be a victim. Harvey is a photographer, and the first time he discovered someone posting his photos was about three years ago when his account was really taking off. It's happened a few times since then.

Sometimes it's just obnoxious, where people are "spammy, or just impersonating." But sometimes, it's much more than that. "The aggravating time was more malicious. Like, someone pretending to be a friend in a really condescending, rude way. It was the type of thing that if misinterpreted as real, could do some real damage."

Instagram doesn't have a mechanism for letting users know it's investigating bogus accounts, and doesn't tell people when, or if, those accounts are deleted.

Instagram is the most common platform photographers, clients and models use to meet and follow each other. Recently though, accounts are getting shut down and mine, with an awesome followers, was among them.

A question I find myself asking is if the investment of building a following on Instagram was worth it. Maybe putting all the eggs in one basket wasn't the wisest decision.

According to Instagram, profanity, spam, using fake likes and nudity are reasons for an account to get shut down. Whether or not these standards have a place in our society is a conversation for another time.

So the question remains: why was the account shut down?

If I had to guess, this most likely happened because people

abused the reporting tool. If this is the case, this opens the door for photographer's (or any other business's) competitors to just report another business and have them removed. All of a sudden the reporting tool becomes a marketing tool. How great would it be if you report your competitor's page enough times to have it shut down?

In an over-populated sea, you just bought yourself some space to stretch out your hands. Instagram is the place where companies and individuals can check out your work, see how you interact with followers, and learn about the product you offer. If you wipe out a competitor by simply reporting the account, you no longer have to worry that your clients are looking at other pages for ideas, inspiration or services.

To access Instagram's terms and conditions you can click here or just type it on google. But I will discuss some of the things mentioned the Instagram terms and conditions that are worth mentioning.

"You may not post violent, nude, partially nude, discriminatory, unlawful, infringing, hateful, pornographic or sexually suggestive photos or other content via the Service."

You will always have some people very vocal about the opinions in a not very well mannered way but before reacting to any negative comments, you have to think about your business and about the fact that not everyone is going to love your business and your account. Some people like criticizing or giving you unsolicited advice on your account even when they haven't achieved anything. You don't need their opinion and should just ignore them. Your time is far too precious to waste it on them.

" You may not use the Service for any illegal or unauthorized purpose. You agree to comply with all laws, rules and regulations (for example, federal, state, local and provincial) applicable to your use of the Service and your Content (defined below), including but not limited to, copyright laws."

I think the most important thing here is the copyright part. Before publishing anything that hasn't been created by you, make sure you do your research about the copyright aspect.

"You must not create accounts with the Service through unauthorized means, including but not limited to, by using an automated device, script, bot, spider, crawler or scraper."

This refers to getting followers using an automated software o website. First of all, you don't need those type of followers because they will not care about your account and might not even have an interest in your niche. The best way and the only way you should get followers in in an organic way, by engaging with them. If people are not actually interested and engaged with you, they will not buy or participate in anything related to your business, regardless how many followers you have. Sometimes is not just about the numbers; it's about the quality of the followers. When using your account for all the services mentioned in the previous section, the rate of engagement is going to be much hight when your account is built on trust and friendship. This will make the customers happy that their products are selling and will bring even more business your way.

Here is the scariest one of all of the Instagram Terms and conditions:

"We reserve the right to modify or terminate the Service or your access to the Service for any reason, without notice, at any time, and without liability to you. "

This has happened to some users and it's not pleasant. You work hard and someday you wake up that your account has been shot down. All I can say is just make sure that you are doing the right thing at all times and this will not happen. Another thing that you can do (I always like to think of plan b), is to open an account in a similar niche and to send your followers there too, in case one goes away, you have the other one. For example, if you have an account that is focused on pets, you can divide your audience and ope two more accounts focused on cat lover or dog lovers. If you have an account focusing on Yoga, you can direct your followers towards hot yoga, now you get the point.

Conclusion

After reading this book, you have gained great insight on the Instagram platform. The book started by teaching you how to set up your account in a successful way and how to grow it gradually so that you can gain quality followers that care about you and your niche.

After getting to a stage where you have a significant number of followers, there are at least 19 ways in which you can put those followers to use to bring you an income.

I have taken it one step further and advised you to build a website and even a consultancy business using your Instagram account, once it has reached a significant number of followers.

The last chapter has also taught you how to keep your Instagram account by only uploading quality content and photos and only promote products that you have tested and you truly believe in. At this stage, you have acquired a great amount of knowledge and I hope that you will put it into practice very soon.

Thank you very much for reading this book. If you have enjoyed this book and you feel that was useful, please leave a review and maybe get in touch to let me know how your Instagram business in doing.